Spirit
of
Leadership

Inspiring Quotations for Leaders

Spirit
of
Leadership
Inspiring Quotations for Leaders

Complied by Frederick C. Harrison

LEADERSHIP EDUCATION AND DEVELOPMENT, INC.
GERMANTOWN, TN.

Published by Leadership Education and Development, Inc.,
P.O. Box 3820007, Germantown, TN 38138-2007.

Although the publisher has exhaustively researched all sources to ensure the accuracy and completeness of the information contained in this book, we assume no responsibility for errors, inaccuracies, omissions or any inconsistency herein.

First Edition, 1989
Printed in the United States of America

Library of Congress Cataloging-in-Publication Data

Spirit of leadership.

   Includes index.
   1. Leadership—Quotations, maxims, etc. I. Harrison, Frederick C.,
PN6084.L15S6   1989   082   89-2498
ISBN O-943703-02-6

Contents

Contents

Introduction

One of the great joys of life is discovering new insights into human nature in general and yourself in particular. From the observations of poets, statesmen, writers and business executives comes a wealth of wisdom that provides understanding, guidance and inspiration for leaders or potential leaders in all walks of life.

In this book you will learn from the likes of Emerson, Twain, Lincoln, Churchill, Schweitzer, Franklin, Edison, Peale, Iacocca and many others. You will find that their words speak to you or have relevance for you in different ways as conditions and situations change in your life. At one time, a saying may lead you to discover an important truth about yourself, strengthen a conviction, or reinforce an important value. At another time, the words may inspire you to take bold action to resolve a difficult problem.

Refer often to the treasury of quotations found on the following pages. Memorize those that are most meaningful to you. Most of all, enjoy the feelings expressed. For as William Ellery Channing tells us:

> Quotations are true levelers. They give to all who will faithfully use them the spiritual presence of the best and greatest of the human race.

1

Leadership Ideals

Ideas go booming through the world louder than cannons. Thoughts are mightier than armies. Principles have achieved more victories than horsemen or chariots.
                                        W.M. Paxton

Ideals are like stars; you will not succeed in touching them with your hands. But like the seafaring man on the desert of waters, you choose them as your guides, and following them you will reach your destiny.
                                        Carl Schurz

Back of every noble life there are principles that have fashioned it.
                                        George H. Lorimer

In matters of principle, stand like a rock.
Thomas Jefferson

Never waiver from your deeply rooted values.

It is not the strength, but the duration, of great sentiments that makes great men.
Friedrich Nietzsche

Strong convictions precede great actions.
Author Unknown

The time is always right to do what is right.

> Martin Luther King, Jr.

It is not who is right, but what is right, that is of importance.

> Thomas Huxley

A reputation for a thousand years may depend upon the conduct of a single moment.

> Ernest Bramah

Have regard for your name since it will remain with you forever.

The first step in the evolution of ethics is a sense of solidarity with other human beings.

Albert Schweitzer

No man can live happily who regards himself alone, who turns everything to his own advantage. You must live for others if you wish to live for yourself.

Seneca

Compassion is the basis of all morality.
Arthur Schopenhauer

Toleration is the greatest gift of the mind.
Helen Keller

Faith in the ability of a leader is of slight service unless it be united with faith in his justice.
George B. Goethals

I believe the first test of a truly great man is humility.
John Ruskin

Half of the harm that is done in this world is due to people who want to feel important... they do not mean to do harm... they are absorbed in the endless struggle to think well of themselves.

T. S. Eliot

Conceit is the quicksand of success.

Arnold Glasow

The bigger a man's head gets, the easier it is to fill his shoes.

Henry A. Courtney

The superior man is modest in his speech but exceeds in his actions.

Confucius

Pride is at the bottom of all great mistakes.

John Ruskin

If I had only one sermon to preach, it would be a sermon against pride.

Gilbert K. Chesterton

Any man worth his salt will stick up for what he believes right, but it takes a slightly bigger man to acknowledge instantly and without reservation that he is in error.

Gen. Peyton C. March

There are no mistakes so great as that of being always right.

Samuel Butler

Truth is the strongest and most powerful weapon a man can use, whether he is fighting for a reform or fighting for a sale.

Arthur Dunn

Set the course of your life by the three stars — sincerity, courage and unselfishness. From these flow a host of other virtues... He who follows them will obtain the highest type of success, that which lies in the esteem of others.

Dr. Monroe E. Deutsch

There is one element that is worth its weight in gold and that is loyalty. It will cover a multitude of weaknesses.

Phillip Armour

There is no road too long to the man who advances deliberately and without undue haste; no honors too distant to the man who prepares himself for them with patience.

Bruyers

Genius is eternal patience.

Michaelangelo

11

Have patience with all things, but chiefly have patience with yourself. Do not lose courage in considering your own imperfections, but instantly set about remedying them. Everyday begin the task anew.

Saint Francis de Sales

Have patience, all things are difficult before they become easy.

Saadi

Things may come to those who wait, but only the things left by those who hustle.

Abraham Lincoln

The kind of people I look for to fill top management spots are the eager beavers. These are the guys who do more than expected — they always reach.

Lee Iacocca

It is always the adventurous who accomplish great things.

Montesquieu

Too many executives tend to follow the road proved safe rather than the dynamic approach of self-reliance, individualism and initiative.

Louis E. Wolfson

I could not tread these perilous paths in safety, if I did not keep a saving sense of humor.

Lord Nelson

What we do upon some great occasion will probably depend on what we already are: and what we are will be the result of previous years of self-discipline.

H. P. Liddon

The four-way test of the things we think, say or do:
    ...Is it the truth?
    ...Is it fair to all concerned?
    ...Will it build good will and better
        relationships?
    ...Will it be beneficial to all concerned?

Rotary International Motto

RESOLUTION

Whereas the Supreme Power of the universe has deemed it natural to create human beings of various colors, races, and creeds; and

Whereas in his sight they all are his equally beloved children;

Therefore be it resolved that there is no superior race or group of peoples and that all men are brothers of equal rank; and be it further resolved that we know this and believe it now and forever!

W. Newman

Even the hint of prejudice of any type has no place in a well run organization.

Fred A. Manske, Jr.

2

Leadership Style

Outstanding leaders appeal to the hearts of their followers — not their minds.

The ideal leadership style — power based on competence and admiration.

Leadership is action, not position.
Donald H. McGannon

Those that create, lead!

The ultimate leader is one who is willing to develop people to the point that they eventually surpass him or her in knowledge and ability.

Fred A. Manske, Jr.

Effective leaders bring out the best in people by stimulating them to achieve what they thought was impossible.

Effective leaders make their followers feel good about themselves and their work.

A leader is best when people barely know he exists... when his work is done, his aim fulfilled, they will say, "We did this ourselves."

Lao-tzu

The final test of a leader is that he leaves behind in other people the convictions and the will to carry on.

Walter Lippmann

One of the most important maxims of leadership is: Be there with your personnel.

One of the problems of American corporations is the reluctance of managers to practice visible management—to get out and listen and talk to employees.

Ed Carlson

The desk is a dangerous place from which to watch the world.

John le Carré

"Management by wandering around," may be the most important thing managers can do to improve work quality and productivity.

Thomas Peters and Robert H. Waterman, Jr.
In Search of Excellence

It is not fair to ask of others what you are not willing to do yourself.

Eleanor Roosevelt

A great leader never sets himself above his followers except in carrying responsibilities.

Jules Ormont

A true leader always keeps an element of surprise up his sleeve, which others cannot grasp but which keeps his public excited and breathless.

Charles de Gaulle

Occasionally, it's necessary for the leader to be unpredictable and inconsistent. If you're too predictable some people will take advantage of you.

The best leader is the one who has the sense to surround himself with outstanding people and the self-restraint not to meddle with how they do their jobs.

Never tell people how to do things. Tell them what to do and they will surprise you with their ingenuity.

Gen. George Patton, Jr.

Effective leaders have the ability to boil down complex issues into concise, straightforward statements of what should be done.

Genius is the ability to reduce the complicated to the simple.

C. W. Ceran

If you command wisely, you'll be obeyed cheerfully.

Thomas Fuller

3

Vision

The empires of the future are empires of the mind.

Winston Churchill

Nothing happens unless first a dream.

Carl Sandburg

The only limits are, as always, those of vision.

James Broughton

All men who have achieved great things have been dreamers.

Orison Swett Marden

The most successful leader of all is the one who sees another picture not yet actualized.
Mary Parker Follett

Cherish your visions and your dreams as they are the children of your soul; the blue prints of your ultimate achievements.
Napoleon Hill

He who cherishes a beautiful vision, a lofty ideal in his heart, will one day realize it.
James Allen

The future belongs to those who believe in the beauty of their dreams.

Eleanor Roosevelt

Keep true to the dreams of your youth.

Johann Schiller

Outstanding leaders are future-oriented. They love to dream about what could be and to involve others in their dreams.

31

Like small creeks that grow into mighty rivers, the dreams of leaders eventually shape the course of history.

Some men see things as they are and say "Why?" I dream things that never were, and say, "Why not?"

George Bernard Shaw

Look at things as they can be.

David J. Schwartz

*A rock pile ceases to be a rock pile the
moment a single man contemplates it,
bearing within him the image of a cathedral.*
Saint-Exupéry

*Performance breakthroughs come from
pondering the unthinkable.*

Big thinking precedes great achievement.
Wilferd A. Peterson

Ideas control the world.

James A. Garfield

4

Excellence

Excellence is best described as doing the right things right—selecting the most important things to be done and then accomplishing them 100% correctly.

Every job is a self-portrait of the person who did it. Autograph your work with excellence!

Commitment To Excellence

Anybody who accepts mediocrity—in school, on the job, in life—is a person who compromises, and when the leader compromises, the whole organization compromises.

Charles Knight

It's a funny thing about life: if you refuse to accept anything but the very best you will very often get it.

Somerset Maugham

Good enough is the enemy of excellence.

Everything can be improved.

C. W. Barron

No one ever attains very eminent success by simply doing what is required of him; it is the amount and excellence of what is over and above the required that determines greatness.

Charles Kendall Adams

Here is a simple but powerful rule: Always give people more than they expect to get.

Nelson Boswell

Hold yourself responsible for a higher standard than anybody else expects of you.

Henry Ward Beecher

People forget how fast you did a job—but they remember how well you did it.

Howard W. Newton

It is quality rather than quantity that matters.

Seneca

Quality is never an accident; it is always the result of high intentions, sincere effort, intelligent direction and skillful execution; it represents the wise choice of many alternatives.

Willa A. Foster

Great leaders are never satisfied with current levels of performance. They are restlessly driven by possibilities and potential achievements.

Donna Harrison

Progress is not created by contented people.

F. Tyger

This became a credo of mine... attempt the impossible in order to improve your work.

Bette Davis

All glory comes from daring to begin.
William Shakespeare

Great things are not done by impulse but by a series of small things brought together.
Vincent Van Gogh

Don't be afraid to give your best to what seemingly are small jobs. Every time you conquer one it makes you that much stronger. If you do the little jobs well, the big ones tend to take care of themselves.
Dale Carnegie

Of all things a leader should fear complacency heads the list.

A small leak will sink a great ship.
                                    Thomas Fuller

Permissiveness is the neglect of duty.
                                    Zig Ziglar

As a manager you're paid to be uncomfortable. If you're comfortable, it's a sure sign you're doing things wrong.
                                    Peter Drucker

5

Servant Leadership

The image of George Washington kneeling in prayer at Valley Forge says something about the method of all leadership — humble, modest service.

George Sweeting

The noblest service comes from nameless hands. And the best servant does his work unseen.

Oliver Wendell Holmes

There is no more noble occupation in the world than to assist another human being — to help someone succeed.

Alan Loy McGinnis

The service we render to others is really the rent we pay for our room on this earth. It is obvious that man is himself a traveller; that the purpose of this world is not "to have and to hold" but "to give and serve." There can be no other meaning.

Sir Wilfred T. Grenfell

What do we live for, if it is not to make life less difficult for each other?

George Eliot

No one is useless in this world who lightens the burdens of another.

Charles Dickens

The sole meaning of life is to serve humanity.

Tolstoi

Of those to whom much is given, much is required.

John F. Kennedy

What we have done for ourselves alone dies with us. What we have done for others and the world remains and is immortal.

Albert Pine

Try to forget yourself in the service of others. For when we think too much of ourselves and our own interests, we easily become despondent. But when we work for others, our efforts return to bless us.

Sidney Powell

We cannot hold a torch to light another's path without brightening our own.

Ben Sweetland

The great paradox of life: The more you give of yourself, the more you receive.

Half of the world is on the wrong scent in the pursuit of happiness. They think it consists in having and getting, and in being served by others. It consists in giving and serving others.

Henry Drummond

The only ones among you who will be really happy are those who will have sought and found how to serve.

Albert Schweitzer

Build a reservoir of good will by placing the interests of your people above your own.

Effective leaders follow the basic dictum of a West Pointer: Make sure the troops are settled and fed before you take care of your own needs.

Who has not served cannot command.
John Florio

6

Power

There is no meaning to life except the meaning man gives his life by the unfolding of his powers.

Erich Fromm

The greatest contribution leaders can make to mankind is to use their power in a positive way — to help and inspire others.

Fred A. Manske, Jr.

The measure of a man is what he does with power.

Pittacus

If a man can accept a situation in a place of power with the thought that it's only temporary, he comes out all right. But when he thinks he is the cause of the power, that can be his ruination.

Harry S. Truman

Most powerful is he who has himself in his power.

Lucius Annaeus Seneca

Nearly all men can stand adversity, but if you want to test a man's character, give him power.

Abraham Lincoln

Corruption and dishonesty seem to occur when the leader loses sight of the fact that he or she is given power for one purpose — to serve others.

Power for good flows through you from God. It does not originate with you.

W. F. Smith

I often say of George Washington that he was one of the few in the whole history of the world who was not carried away by power.

Robert Frost

Power may justly be compared to a great river; while kept within its bounds it is both beautiful and useful, but when it overflows its banks, it brings destruction and desolation to all in its way.

Andrew Hamilton

7

Responsibility

The price of greatness is responsibility.
                                    Winston Churchill

I believe that every right implies a responsibility; every opportunity, an obligation; every possession, a duty.
                                    John D. Rockefeller, Jr.

He who is false to the present duty breaks a thread in the loom, and you will see the effect when the weaving of a lifetime is unraveled.
                                    Ellery Channing

You can't escape the responsibility of tomorrow by evading it today.
                                    Abraham Lincoln

The ability to accept responsibility is the measure of the man.

Roy L. Smith

The one quality that all successful people have is the ability to take on responsibility.

Michael Korda

The day you take complete responsibility for yourself, the day you stop making excuses, that's the day you start to the top.

O. J. Simpson

It is not enough that we do our best; sometimes we have to do what's required.

Winston Churchill

We have all a few moments in life of hard glorious running; but we have days and years of walking — the uneventful discharge of small duties.

Alexander MacLaren

There are no office hours for leaders.

Cardinal Gibbons

If you can't stand the heat, stay out of the kitchen.

Harry S. Truman

8

Character

Character is destiny.

Heraclitus

Character is the indelible mark that determines the only true value of all people and all their work.

Orison Swett Marden

Character is power; it makes friends, draws patronage and support and opens the way to wealth, honor and happiness.

J. Howe

Character is the foundation stone upon which one must build to win respect. Just as no worthy building can be erected on a weak foundation, so no lasting reputation worthy of respect can be built on a weak character.

R. C. Samsel

No man can climb out beyond the limitations of his own character.

John Morley

A good name is seldom regained. When character is gone, one of the richest jewels of life is lost forever.

J. Hanes

How a man plays the game shows something of his character; how he loses shows all of it.

Camden County, Georgia **Tribune**

Good character is more to be praised than outstanding talent. Most talents are to some extent a gift. Good character, by contrast, is not given to us. We have to build it piece by piece — by thought, choice, courage and determination.

John Luther

You can not dream yourself into a character; you must hammer and forge yourself one.
James A. Froude

69

Small kindnesses, small courtesies, and small considerations habitually practiced in our social intercourse give a greater charm to the character than the display of great talent and accomplishments.

Kelty

By constant self-discipline and self-control you can develop greatness of character.

Grenville Kleiser

The law of harvest is to reap more than you sow. Sow an act, and you reap a habit; sow a habit, and you reap a character; sow a character and you reap a destiny.

G. D. Boardman

9

Honesty

An honest man is the noblest work of God.
Alexander Pope

No legacy is so rich as honesty.
William Shakespeare

The first step in greatness is to be honest.
Samuel Johnson

Honesty is the first chapter of the book of wisdom.
Thomas Jefferson

To many a man, and sometimes to a youth, there comes the opportunity to choose between honorable competence and tainted wealth... The young man who starts out poor and honorable holds in his hand one of the strongest elements of success.
Orison Swett Marden

I hope I shall possess firmness and virtue enough to maintain what I consider the most enviable of all titles, the character of an honest man.

George Washington

Each time you are honest and conduct yourself with honesty, a success force will drive you toward greater success. Each time you lie, even with a little white lie, there are strong forces pushing you toward failure.

Joseph Sugarman

10

Integrity

The supreme quality for a leader is unquestionably integrity. Without it, no real success is possible, no matter whether it is on a section gang, a football field, in an army or in an office.

Dwight D. Eisenhower

Integrity is the glue that holds our way of life together.

Billy Graham

You are already of consequence in the world if you are known as a man of strict integrity.

Grenville Kleiser

People of integrity expect to be believed. They also know time will prove them right and are willing to wait.

Ann Landers

The key question you must always ask yourself: "What is the right thing to do?"

Keep true, never be ashamed of doing right; decide on what you think is right and stick to it.

George Eliot

To see what is right, and not to do it, is want of courage.

Confucius

A person is not given integrity. It results from the relentless pursuit of honesty at all times.

Integrity is not a given in everyone's life. It is the result of self-discipline, inner trust and a decision to be relentlessly honest in all situations in our lives.

Workman 1987 Page-A-Day Calendar

11

Enthusiasm

II

Enthusiasm

Every great and commanding moment in the annals of the world is the triumph of some enthusiasm.

Ralph Waldo Emerson

Enthusiasm is the electric current that keeps the engine of life going at top speed. Enthusiasm is the very propeller of progress.

B. C. Forbes

Enthusiasm is the greatest asset — more than power or influence or money.

Author Unknown

If you can give your son only one gift, let it be enthusiasm.

Bruce Barton

One man has enthusiasm for 30 minutes, another for 30 days, but it is the man who has it for 30 years who makes a success of his life.

Edward B. Butler

Like the chicken and the egg, enthusiasm and success seem to go together. We suspect, however, that enthusiasm comes first. If you hope to succeed at anything in this world, polish up your enthusiasm and hang on to it.

John Luther

No one keeps up his enthusiasm automatically. Enthusiasm must be nourished with new actions, new aspirations, new efforts, new vision. It is one's own fault if his enthusiasm is gone; he has failed to feed it.

Papyrus

12

Positive Attitude

The most positive men are the most credulous.

Alexander Pope

Exhilaration of life can be found only with an upward look. This is an exciting world. It is cram-packed with opportunity. Great moments wait around every corner.

Richard M. Devos

The greatest discovery of my generation is that man can alter his life style simply by altering his attitude of mind.

William James

Three men were laying brick.
The first was asked, "What are you doing?"
He answered, "Laying some brick."
The second man was asked, "What are
*   you working for?"*
He answered, "Five dollars a day."
The third man was asked, "What are you
*   doing?"*
He answered, "I am helping to build a
*   great Cathedral."*
Which man are you?

Charles M. Schwab

No one ever finds life worth living—he
has to make it worth living

Author Unknown

90

Nothing can stop the man with the right mental attitude from achieving his goal; nothing on earth can help the man with the wrong mental attitude.

W. W. Ziege

We can not tell what may happen to us in the strange medley of life. But we can decide what happens in us—how we take it, what we do with it—and that is what really counts in the end.

Joseph F. Newton

You can not always control circumstances, but you can control your own thoughts.

Charles Popplestown

Whatever is true, whatever is honorable, whatever is just, whatever is pure, whatever is lovely, whatever is gracious… think about these things.

Bible, *Phillipians 4:8*

If you look for the positive things in life, you'll find them.

Life is a one-way street. No matter how many detours you take, none of them leads back. And once you know and accept that, life becomes much simpler.

Isabel Moore

Therefore do not be anxious about tomorrow, for tomorrow will be anxious for itself. Let the day's own trouble be sufficient for the day.

Bible, *Matthew 6:34*

If you will call your troubles experiences, and remember that every experience develops some latent force within you, you will grow vigorous and happy, however adverse your circumstances may seem to be.

John R. Miller

Keep your face to the sunshine and you cannot see the shadow.

Helen Keller

Cultivate optimism by committing yourself to a cause, a plan or a value system. You'll feel that you are growing in a meaningful direction which will help you rise above day-to-day setbacks.

Dr. Robert Conroy
Bottom Line-Personal

If you can dream it, you can do it.

Walt Disney

13

Courage

Courage is the first of human qualities because it is the quality which guarantees all others.

Winston Churchill

The ultimate measure of a man is not where he stands in moments of comfort and convenience, but where he stands at times of challenge and controversy.

Martin Luther King, Jr.

The ideal man bears the accidents of life with dignity and grace, making the best of circumstances.

Aristotle

I love the man that can smile in trouble, that can gather strength from distress, and grow brave by reflections.

Thomas Paine

There is nothing in the world so much admired as a man who knows how to bear unhappiness with courage.

Seneca

Greatness, in the last analysis, is largely bravery — courage in escaping from old ideas and old standards and respectable ways of doing things.

James Harvey Robinson

Success is never final and failure never fatal. It's courage that counts.

George F. Tilton

You will never do anything worthwhile in this world without courage.

James Allen

I am convinced that one of the biggest factors in success is the courage to undertake something.

James A. Worsham

Don't be afraid to go out on a limb. That's where the fruit is.

Soundings

If I were asked to give what I consider the single most useful bit of advice it would be this: Expect trouble as an inevitable part of life and when it comes, hold your head high, look it squarely in the eye and say "I will be bigger than you. You can not defeat me."

Ann Landers

March on. Fear not the thorns or the sharp stones on life's path.

Kahlil Gibran

Great trials seem to be a necessary preparation for great duties.

Thompson

The gem cannot be polished without friction, nor man perfected without trials.

Chinese Proverb

14

Determination

He conquers who endures.

Persius

An invincible determination can accomplish almost anything and in this lies the great distinction between great men and little men.

Thomas Fuller

Nothing is impossible to a willing heart.

John Heywood

Most people give up just when they're about to achieve success. They quit on the one yard line. They give up at the last minute of the game one foot from a winning touchdown.

H. Ross Perot

Never, never, never quit.

Winston Churchill

Defeat never comes to any man until he admits it.

Joseph Daniels

Your mind can amaze your body if you just keep telling yourself, I can do it, I can do it, I can do it!

Jon Erickson

If you think you can, or you think you can't, your probably right.

Mark Twain

When nothing seems to help, I go and look at a stonecutter hammering away at his rock perhaps a hundred times without as much as a crack showing in it. Yet at the hundred and first blow it will split in two and I know it was not that blow that did it — but all that had gone before.

Jacob Riis

In all human affairs there are efforts, and there are results, and the strength of effort is the measure of the result.

James Allen

Let me tell you the secret that has led me to my goal. My strength lies solely in my tenacity.

Louis Pasteur

Bear in mind, if you are going to amount to anything, that your success does not depend upon the brilliancy and the impetuosity with which you take hold, but upon the ever lasting and sanctified bulldoggedness with which you hang on after you have taken hold.

Dr. A. B. Meldrum

We can do anything we want to do if we stick to it long enough.

Helen Keller

Every worthwhile accomplishment, big or little, has its stages of drudgery and triumph; a beginning, a struggle and a victory.

Author Unknown

Any man can work when every stroke of his hand brings down the fruit rattling from the tree to the ground; but to labor in season and out of season, under every discouragement, by the power of truth — that requires a heroism which is transcendent.

Henry Ward Beecher

The heights by great men reached and kept were not obtained by sudden flight, but they, while their companions slept, were toiling upward in the night.

Henry Wadsworth Longfellow

Perseverance is not a long race; it is many short races one after another.

Walter Elliott

Little strokes fell great oaks.

Ben Franklin

PRESS ON. Nothing in the world can take the place of persistence. Talent will not; nothing is more common than unsuccessful men with talent. Genius will not; rewarded genius is a proverb. Education will not; the world is full of educated derelicts.

Persistence and determination alone are omnipotent.

Calvin Coolidge

15

Ambition

*Aim at the sun, and you may not reach it;
but your arrow will fly far higher than if
you aimed at an object on a level with
yourself.*

J. Howse

*Far away there in the sunshine are my
highest aspirations. I may not reach them,
but I can look up and see their beauty,
believe in them and try to follow where
they lead.*

Louisa May Alcott

*You will become as small as your con-
trolling desire; as great as your dominant
aspiration.*

James Allen

Make no little plans. They have no magic to stir men's blood. Make big plans: aim high.

D. H. Burnham

Don't be afraid to take a big step if one is indicated. You can't cross a chasm in two small jumps.

David Lloyd George

Do not follow where the path may lead. Go instead where there is no path and leave a trail.

Motivational Quotes

Take the course opposite to custom and you will almost always do well.

Jean Jacques Rousseau

The greater the obstacle, the more glory in overcoming it.

Moliére

Destiny is not a matter of chance, it is a matter of choice; it is not a thing to be waited for, it is a thing to be achieved.

William Jennings Bryan

Resolve that whatever you do you will bring the whole man to it; that you will fling the whole weight of your being into it.

Orison Swett Marden

115

Unless you are willing to drench yourself in your work beyond the capacity of the average man, you are just not cut out for positions at the top.

J. C. Penney

There has never yet been a man in our history who led a life of ease whose name is worth remembering.

Theodore Roosevelt

Show me a thoroughly satisfied man — and I will show you a failure.

Thomas Edison

To make it to the top, you've got to want it with all your heart.

Linda Wachman

Each day you have to look into the mirror and say to yourself, "I'm going to be the best I can no matter what it takes."

Barbara Jordon

…Let your heart soar as high as it will. Refuse to be average.

A. W. Tozer

16

Setting The Example

To set a lofty example is the richest bequest a man can leave behind him.

S. Smiles

Example is the school of mankind and they will learn at no other.

Edmond Burke

Example is not the main thing in influencing others. It is the only thing.

Albert Schweitzer

The first great gift we can bestow on others is a good example.

Thomas Morell

People are changed, not by coercion or intimidation, but by example.

A man who lives right, and is right, has more power in his silence than another has by his words.

Phillips Brooks

Honesty and integrity are best taught by example.

More than anything else followers want to believe that their leaders are ethical and honest. They want to say, "Someday I want to be like him or her."

People never improve unless they look to some standard or example higher and better than themselves.

Tryon Edwards

The speed of the boss is the speed of the team.

Lee Iacocca

You must set the standards!

Charles H. Kellstadt

17

Inspiring Employees

Techniques don't produce quality products or pick up the garbage on time; people do, people who care, people who are treated as creatively contributing adults.

Tom Peters

The best way to gain and hold the loyalty of your personnel is to show interest in them and care for them, by your words and actions, in everything you do.

People are not motivated by failure; they are motivated by achievement and recognition.

F. F. Fournies

The opportunity to accomplish challenging tasks inspires people to give their best.

Innovation thrives on encouragement.
Author Unknown

Few things in the world are more powerful than a positive push. A smile. A word of optimism and hope. A "you can do it" when things are tough.

Richard M. Devos

A word of encouragement during a failure is worth more than a whole book of praise after a success.

Bits & Pieces

To do something, however small, to make others happier and better is the highest ambition, the most elevating hope, which can inspire a human being.

John Lubbock

There is no investment you can make which will pay you so well as the effort to scatter sunshine and good cheer through your establishment.

Orison Swett Marden

Outstanding leaders go out of the way to boost the self-esteem of their personnel. If people believe in themselves, its amazing what they can accomplish.

Sam Walton

Well led followers feel useful, important and part of a worthwhile enterprise.

When people are made to feel secure and important and appreciated, it will no longer be necessary for them to whittle down others in order to seem bigger in comparison.

Virginia Arcastle

The deepest principle in human nature is the craving to be appreciated.

William James

People thrive on the appreciation you show them — the smiles, the thanks and the gestures of kindness.

Appreciative words are the most powerful force for good on earth!

George W. Crane

Catch your people doing something right and let them know you appreciate it.

If each of us were to confess his most secret desire, the one that inspires all his plans, all his actions, he would say: "I want to be praised."

E. M. Cioran

Most of us, swimming against tides of trouble the world knows nothing about, need only a bit of praise or encouragement —and we'll make the goal.

Jerome P. Fleishman

A word of praise is far more meaningful to a person if it is related to one of his or her qualities (such as enthusiasm, intelligence, positive attitude or integrity) than if it is tied to performance results.

If anything goes bad, I did it. If anything goes semi-good, then we did it. If anything goes real good, then you did it. That's all it takes to get people to win football games for you.

Bear Bryant

The very essence of all power to influence lies in getting the other person to participate.

Harry A. Overstreet

Involvement leads to commitment.

People support what they help to create.

Author Unknown

What gets rewarded, gets done.

If you expect the best from your personnel, more than likely you will get it.

Getting a fair deal is the most important concern to employees at all levels.

Morale and productivity are highest in work groups when the leader shows a high degree of consideration and concern for employees.

Handle an employee's problem swiftly and as seriously as if it were a problem with your own paycheck.

Trust is the emotional glue that binds followers and leaders together.

Warren Bennis & Bert Nanus,
Leaders

Few things help an individual more than to place responsibility upon him, and to let him know you trust him.

Booker T. Washington

The highest compliment a leader can receive is one that is given by the people who work for him.

James L. Barksdale

18

Communicating Effectively

Nine-tenths of the serious controversies that arise in life result from misunderstanding, from one man not knowing the facts which to the other man seem important, or otherwise failing to appreciate his point of view.

Justice Louis D. Brandeis

Free and fair discussion will ever be found the firmest friend to truth.

G. Campbell

Leaders who make it a practice to draw out the thoughts and ideas of their subordinates and who are receptive even to bad news will be properly informed.

Communicate downward to subordinates with at least the same care and attention as you communicate upward to superiors.

L. B. Belker

The basic building block of good communications is the feeling that every human being is unique and of value.

The finest expression of respect is not praise or status, but a willingness to talk openly to a person.

Less Bittle

The most important good listening habit is to totally concentrate on what the person is saying.

When the employees no longer believe that their manager listens to them, they start looking around for someone who will.

19

Developing
Subordinates

The growth and development of people is the highest calling of leadership.

It is only as we develop others that we permanently succeed.

Harvey S. Firestone

Give a man a fish, and you feed him for a day. Teach a man to fish, and you feed him for a lifetime.

Chinese Proverb

Treat people as if they were what they ought to be and you help them to become what they are capable of being.

Goethe

Those who believe in our ability do more than stimulate us. They create for us an atmosphere in which it becomes easier to succeed.

John H. Spalding

Create the kind of climate in your organization where personal growth is expected, recognized and rewarded.

The role of the coach is to teach his players to stand on their own feet.

Good leadership consists in showing average people how to do the work of superior people.

John D. Rockefeller

A development-oriented leader pushes people beyond the threshold of their self-imposed limits toward their own unrealized potential.

Lyman Wood

Encourage your personnel to explore new options instead of settling for the obvious.

If your subordinates aren't making an occasional mistake or two, it's a sure sign they're playing it too safe.

A young branch takes on all the bends that one gives it.

Chinese Proverb

The true secret of giving advice is, after you have honestly given it, to be perfectly indifferent whether it is taken or not.

Hannah W. Smith

20

Decision Making

Successful leaders have the courage to take action where others hesitate.

Even though you're on the right track — you'll get run over if you just sit there.

Will Rogers

Again and again the impossible problem is solved when we see that the problem is only a tough decision waiting to be made.

Dr. Robert H. Schuller

151

Your decisions will always be better if you do what is right for the organization rather than what is right for yourself.

Take time to deliberate, but when the time for action arrives, stop thinking and go in.
Andrew Jackson

It is better to err on the side of daring than the side of caution.
Alvin Toffler

Trust your instinct to the end, though you can render no reason.

Ralph Waldo Emerson

Never take anything for granted.

Benjamin Disraeli

21

Time Management

Nothing else, perhaps, distinguishes effective executives as much as their tender loving care of time.

Peter Drucker

Time is your most valuable personal resource. Use it wisely because it can't be replaced.

Most time is wasted, not in hours, but in minutes. A bucket with a small hole in the bottom gets just as empty as a bucket that is deliberately emptied.

Paul J. Meyer

A man who dares to waste one hour of life has not discovered the value of life.

Darwin

Leaders need to realize that they can only bring their special abilities to bear on a few critical success areas at one time.

Peak performing leaders distinguish between job activities that they can control and those that they can't and they concentrate on what they can do.

Robert Kriegel

Performing tasks with high leverage is the key to leadership effectiveness.

The reason most major goals are not achieved is that we spend our time doing second things first.

Robert J. McKain

Disciplined focus is what distinguishes those who make things happen from those that watch things happen.

Do not waste your high energy hours. Invest them where they yield the highest payoff.

The first and most important step in improving the utilization of your time is planning.

He who every morning plans the transactions of the day and follows out that plan, carries a thread that will guide him through the labyrinth of the most busy life.

Victor Hugo

Get into the habit of asking yourself if what you're doing can be handled by someone else.

The art of becoming wise is the art of knowing what to look over.

William James

Punctuality is the soul of business.

Thomas Haliburton

22

Life's Lessons

Live your life each day as you would climb a mountain. An occasional glance toward the summit keeps the goal in mind, but many beautiful scenes are to be observed from each new vantage point. Climb slowly, steadily, enjoying each passing moment, and the view from the summit will serve as a fitting climax for the journey.

Harold V. Melchert

Yesterday is a cancelled check; tomorrow is a promissory note; today is the only cash you have—so spend it wisely.

Kay Lyons

Carlyle was right when he said that this life is only a "gleam of light between two eternities." And still some folks take it so hectically and so seriously.

Amos Parrish

Life is a two-stage rocket. The first is physical energy—it ignites and we are off. As physical energy diminishes, the spiritual stage must ignite to boost us into orbit or we will fall back or plateau.

W. F. Smith

Lives of great men all remind us we can make our lives sublime, and departing, leave behind us footprints in the sand of time.

Henry Wadsworth Longfellow

*There is more to life than increasing
its speed.*

Mahatma Gandhi

*I expect to pass through this world but
once. Any good therefore that I can do,
or any kindness that I can show to any
fellow creature, let me do it now. Let me
not defer or neglect it, for I shall not pass
this way again.*

William Penn

*It is the height of absurdity to sow little
but weeds in the first half of one's lifetime
and expect to harvest a valuable crop in
the second half.*

Percy H. Johnston

The harvest of old age is the memory and rich store of blessings laid up earlier in life.
Cicero

Build your "memory bank" now before it is too late to make deposits.

Live now, believe me, wait not till tomorrow; gather the roses of life today.
Pierre de Ronsard

The normal person living to age 70 has 613,200 hours of life. This is too long a period not to have fun.

Did you ever hear someone on his death bed say: "I wish I'd spent more time at the office?"

If your capacity to acquire has outstripped your capacity to enjoy, you are on the way to the scrap-heap.

Glen Buck

If all the gold in the world were melted down into a solid cube it would be about the size of an eight-room house. If a man got possession of all that gold — billions of dollars worth, he could not buy a friend, character, peace of mind, clear conscience or a sense of eternity.

Charles F. Banning

No man can tell whether he is rich or poor by turning to his ledger. It is the heart that makes a man rich. He is rich according to what he is, not according to what he has.

Henry Ward Beecher

For men who matter, life's intangibles have more meaning than the tangibles.

B. C. Forbes

It is where a man spends his money that shows where his heart lies.

A. Edwin Keignin, D.D.

It is the preoccupation with possession, more than anything else, that prevents man from living freely and nobly.
> *Bertrand Russell*

Make money your god, and it will plaque you like the devil.
> *Henry Fielding*

There is no fire like passion, there is no shark like hatred, there is no snare like folly, there is no torrent like greed.
> *Buddha*

Half the harm that is done in this world is due to people who want to feel important.

T. S. Eliot

Many problems in business are caused by the ego interfering with judgement.

There is but a step between a proud man's glory and his disgrace.

Publilius Syrus

The game of life is the game of boomerangs. Our thoughts, deeds and words return to us sooner or later, with astounding accuracy.

Florence Shinn

Our business in life is not to get ahead of others, but to get ahead of ourselves—to break our own records, to outstrip our yesterday by our today, to do our work with more force than ever before.

Stewart B. Johnson

We judge ourselves by what we feel capable of doing, while others judge us by what we have already done.

Henry Wadsworth Longfellow

Whether our efforts are, or are not, favored by life, let us be able to say, when we come near the great goal, I have done what I could.

Louis Pasteur

173

When we have done our best, we should wait the result in peace.

John Lubbock

Nothing on earth consumes a man more completely than the passions of resentment.

Friedrich Nietzsche

He who angers you, conquers you.

Elizabeth Kenny

Life is a battle in which we fall from wounds we receive in running away.

William L. Sullivan

Life is like riding a bicycle. You don't fall off until you stop pedaling.

Claude Pepper

Thy fate is the common fate of all, into each life some rain must fall, some days must be dark and dreary.

Henry Wadsworth Longfellow

Out of every crisis comes the chance to be reborn.

Nena O'Neill

As a man grows older...

> *...He values the voice of experience more and the voice of prophecy less.*

> *...He finds more of life's wealth in the common pleasures — home, health and children.*

> *...He thinks more about the work of men and less about their wealth.*

> *...He begins to appreciate his own father a little more.*

> *...He hurries less, and usually makes more progress.*

> *...He esteems the friendship of God a little higher.*

Roy L. Smith

There is scarcely an instance of a man who has made a fortune by speculation and kept it.

Andrew Carnegie

The habit of saving is itself an education; it fosters every virtue, teaches self-denial and cultivates a sense of order.

T. T. Munger

Those who cannot remember the past are condemned to repeat it.

George Santayana

Many receive advice, only the wise profit from it.

Syrus

Your health must come first. Without it, you have nothing!

A man too busy to take care of his health is like a mechanic too busy to take care of his tools.

Spanish Proverb

Thank God—every morning when you get up—that you have something to do which must be done, whether you like it or not. Being forced to work, and forced to do your best, will breed in you a hundred virtues which the idle never know.

Charles Kingsley

23

Failure

Failure

History has demonstrated that the most notable winners usually encountered heartbreaking obstacles before they triumphed. They finally won because they refused to become discouraged by their defeats.

B. C. Forbes

Remember you will not always win. Some days the most resourceful individuals taste defeat. But there is, in this case, always tomorrow—after you have done your best to achieve success today.

Maxwell Maltz

No man fails who does his best.

Orison Swett Marden

The person interested in success has to learn to view failure as a healthy, inevitable part of the process of getting to the top.

Dr. Joyce Brothers

Our greatest glory is not in never falling, but in rising every time we fall.

Confucius

Failure should challenge us to new heights of accomplishment, not pull us to new depths of despair. Failure is delay, but not defeat. It is temporary detour, not a dead-end street.

William Arthur Ward

The difference between greatness and mediocrity is often how an individual views a mistake.

Nelson Boswell

Failure is the opportunity to begin again more intelligently.

Henry Ford

When defeat comes, accept it as a signal that your plans are not sound. Rebuild those plans and set sail once again toward your coveted goal.

Napoleon Hill

Don't waste energy trying to cover up failure. Learn from your failures and go on to the next challenge. It's OK to fail. If you're not failing, you're not growing.
H. Stanley Judd

Future triumphs are often born from past mistakes.

Sometimes the best gain is to lose.
Herbert

In the game of life it's a good idea to have a few early losses, which relieves you of the pressure of trying to maintain an unde-feated season.
Bill Vaughan

A man is not defeated by his opponents but by himself.

Jan Christian Smuts

The human spirit is never finished when it is defeated... it is finished when it surrenders.

Ben Stein

To expect defeat is nine-tenths of defeat itself.

Francis Crawford

185

I cannot give you the formula for success, but I can give you the formula for failure — which is: try to please everybody.

Herbert Bayard Swope

Failure comes only when we forget our ideals and objectives and principles.

Jawaharal Nehru

24

Happiness

Happiness is not a state to arrive at, but a manner of traveling.

Margaret Lee Runbeck

The supreme happiness of life is the conviction that we are loved.

Victor Hugo

The most glorious moments in your life are not the so-called days of success, but rather those days when out of dejection and despair you feel rise in you a challenge to life, and the promise of future accomplishments.

Gustave Flaubert

Happiness is a by-product of an effort to make someone else happy.

Greta Palmer

Lead the life that will make you kindly and friendly to everyone about you, and you will be surprised what a happy life you will lead.

Charles M. Schwab

The grand essentials of happiness are something to do, something to love, and something to hope for.

Chalmers

Happiness can not be traveled to, owned, earned, worn or consumed. Happiness is the spiritual experience of living every minute with love, grace and gratitude.
                                    Dennis Waitley

To watch the corn grow, or the blossoms set; to draw a hard breath over the plowshare or spade; to read, to think, to love, to pray — these are the things that make men happy.
                                    John Ruskin

Happiness comes of the capacity to feel deeply, to enjoy simply, to think freely, to risk life, to be needed.
                                    Storm Jameson

Satisfaction lies in the effort, not in the attainment. Full effort is full victory.
Mohandas Gandhi

Happiness is essentially a state of going somewhere wholeheartedly without regret or reservation.
William H. Sheldon

Many persons have the wrong idea of what constitutes true happiness. It is not attained through self-gratification but through fidelity to a worthy purpose.
Helen Keller

Real joy comes not from ease or riches or from the praise of men, but from doing something worthwhile.

Sir Wilfred T. Grenfell

The secret of happiness is not in doing what one likes, but in liking what one does.

James M. Barrie

We act as though comfort and luxury were the chief requirements of life, when all that we need to really make us happy is something to be enthusiastic about.

Charles Kingsley

Happiness does not come from doing easy work but from the afterglow of satisfaction that comes after the achievement of a difficult task that demanded our best.

Theodore Rubin

Most people are about as happy as they make up their minds to be.

Abraham Lincoln

25

Faith

Faith is an outward and visible sign of an inward and spiritual grace.
Book of Common Prayer

Faith is the soul's adventure.
William Bridges

Faith is the courage to face reality with hope.
Dr. Robert H. Schuller

As the essence of courage is to stake one's life on a possibility, so the essence of faith is to believe that the possibility exists.
William Salter

If a blade of grass can grown in a concrete walk and a fig tree in the side of a mountain cliff, a human being empowered with an invincible faith can survive all odds the world can throw against his tortured soul.

Dr. Robert H. Schuller

Faith makes all things possible.

Faith of one person in another is the basis of human relationships, in business and all phases of life. People want to know that they can depend on you.

K. C. Ingram

Faith without works is like a bird without wings; though she may hop about on earth, she will never fly to heaven. But when both are joined together, then doth the soul mount up to her eternal rest.

Beaumont

Call, visit or write someone in need every day of your life. Demonstrate your faith by passing it on to someone else.

Dennis Waitley

Associate with people of faith. This tends to be reciprocal. Your faith will communicate itself to them and their faith to you.

Grenville Kleiser

26

Hope

26

Hope

One of the greatest gifts leaders can give others is hope.

Live today well; look to the morrow with vision and hope.

Bonnie Bailey

There is no medicine like hope, no incentive so great, and no tonic so powerful as expectation of something tomorrow.

Orison Swett Marden

The hopeful man sees success where others see failure, sunshine where others see shadows and storm.

Orison Swett Marden

Finish each day and be done with it... you have done what you could; some blunders and absurdities no doubt crept in; forget them as soon as you can. Tomorrow is a new day; you shall begin it well and serenely.

Ralph Waldo Emerson

We should not let our fears hold us back from pursuing our hopes.

John F. Kennedy

He who has health has hope; and he who has hope, has everything.

Arabian Proverb

27

Love

---

*Love is to the heart what the summer is
to the farmer's year. It brings to harvest
all the loveliest flowers of the soul.*

Billy Graham

*Love is an act of endless forgiveness, a
tender look which becomes habit.*

Peter Ustinov

*We are all born for love. It is the principle
of existence, and its only end.*

Benjamin Disraeli

The moment you have in your heart this extra-ordinary thing called love and feel the depth, the delight, the ecstasy of it, you will discover that for you the world is transformed.

J. Krishnamurti

We are all born for love. It is the principle of existence, and its only end.

Benjamin Disraeli

Loving is the only sure road out of darkness the only serum known that cures self-centeredness.

Rod McKuen

What does love look like? It has the hands to help others. It has the feet to hasten to the poor and needy. It has the eyes to see misery and want. It has the ears to hear the sighs and sorrows of men. That is what love looks like.

Saint Augustine

Life without love is like a tree without blossom and fruit.

Kahlil Gibran

Where there is love there is life.

Mohandas Gandhi

There is no fear in love; but perfect love casts out fear.

Bible, *1 John 4:18*

Life in abundance comes only through great love.

Elbert Hubbard

You will find as you look back upon your life that the moments when you have really lived are the moments when you have done things in the spirit of love.

Henry Drummond

Treasure the love you receive above all. It will survive long after your gold and good health have vanished.

O. G. Mandino

Love is like the five loaves and fishes. It doesn't start to multiply until you give it away.

Inspirational Thoughts

Kindness in words creates confidence. Kindness in thinking creates profoundness. Kindness in giving creates love.

Lao-Tzu

*The best portion of a good man's life,
his little nameless, unremembered acts of
kindness and of love.*

William Wordsworth

*Every man feels instinctively that all the
beautiful sentiments in the world weigh
less than a single lovely action.*

James Russell Lowell

*Persons are to be loved; things are to
be used.*

Reuel Howe

Love does not die easily. It is a living thing. It thrives in the face of all life's hazards, save one—neglect.

James D. Bryden

There is no remedy for love but to love more.

Henry David Thoreau

If you want to be loved, be lovable.

Ovid

A father can do nothing better for his children than to love their mother.

Author Unknown

When love and skill work together, expect a masterpiece.

John Ruskin

O Holy Spirit, descend plentifully into my heart. Enlighten the dark corners of this neglected dwelling and scatter there thy cheerful beams.

Saint Augustine

28

Relationships

A relationship is a living thing. It needs and benefits from the same attention to detail that an artist lavishes on his art.

David Viscott
Executive Health

People are lonely because they build walls instead of bridges.

Joseph F. Newton

Real friends warm you with their presence, trust you with their secrets and remember you with their prayers.

Spiritual Reflections

Friendship flourishes at the fountain of forgiveness.

William Arthur Ward

The friendships which last are those wherein each friend respects the other's dignity to the point of not really wanting anything in return.

Cyril Connolly

You can make more friends in two months by becoming really interested in other people than you can in two years by trying to get other people interested in you.

Dale Carnegie

Goodwill is the mightiest practical force in the universe.

Charles Dole

Be kind. Remember everyone you meet is fighting a hard battle.

T. H. Thompson

Constant kindness can accomplish much. As the sun makes ice melt, kindness causes misunderstanding, mistrust and hostility to evaporate.

Albert Schweitzer

No love, no friendship can cross the path of our destiny without leaving some mark on it forever.

Francois Mauriac

29

Possibilities

29

Possibilities

To become what we are capable of becoming is the only end of life.

Spinoza

The only thrill worthwhile is the one that comes from making something out of yourself.

William Feather

The greatest thing in this world is not so much where we are, but in which direction we are moving.

Oliver Wendell Holmes

Few men during their lifetime come any-where near exhausting the resources within them. There are deep wells of strength that are seldom used.

Richard E. Boyd

No one knows what he can do till he tries.

Publilius Syrus

Unless you try to do something beyond what you already mastered, you will never grow.

Ronald Osborn

If you play it safe in life, you've decided that you don't want to grow anymore.
                                          Shirley Hufstedler

All growth is a leap in the dark, a spontaneous unpremeditated act without benefit of experience.

                                          Henry Miller

I've felt that dissatisfaction is the basis of progress. When we become satisfied in business, we become obsolete.
                                          J. Willard Marriott, Sr.

When you're through changing, you're through.

Bruce Barton

People seldom want to walk over you until you lie down.

Elmer Wheeler

Have the daring to accept yourself as a bundle of possibilities and undertake the game of making the most of your best.

Henry Emerson Fosdick

To become different from what we are, we must have some awareness of what we are.

Eric Hoffer

Plant the seeds of expectation in your mind; cultivate thoughts that anticipate achievement. Believe in yourself as being capable of overcoming all obstacles and weaknesses.

Dr. Norman Vincent Peale

Within you right now is the power to do things you never dreamed possible. This power becomes available to you just as soon as you can change your beliefs.

Maxwell Maltz

Life's battles don't always go to the stronger or faster man; but sooner or later the man who wins is the man who thinks he can.
Author Unknown

What you hold in your imagination about yourself, you will become.

When one door closes, another opens; but we often look so long and so regretfully upon the closed door that we do not see the one which has opened for us.
Alexander Graham Bell

Opportunities are usually disguised as hard work, so most people don't recognize them.

Ann Landers

To bring one's self to a frame of mind and to the proper energy to accomplish things that require plain hard work continuously is the one big battle that everyone has. When this battle is won for all time, then everything is easy.

Thomas A. Buckner

Don't wait for your ship to come in, swim out to it.

Motivational Quotes

Be brave enough to live creatively. The creative is the place where no one else has ever been. You have to leave the city of your comfort and go into the wilderness of your intuition. You can't get there by bus, only by hard work, risking and by not quite knowing what you're doing. What you'll discover will be wonderful: yourself.

Alan Alda

30

Self-Development

It is the capacity to develop and improve their skills that distinguishes leaders from their followers.

Warren Bennis and Bert Nanus
Leaders

Leadership development is a life-time journey — not a brief trip.

When an archer misses the mark he turns and looks for the fault within himself. Failure to hit the bull's-eye is never the fault of the target. To improve your aim, improve yourself.

Gilbert Arland

You must take responsibility for your own development.

We will be victorious if we have not forgotten how to learn.

Rosa Luxemburg

Live to learn and you will learn to live.

Portuguese Proverb

Anyone who stops learning is old, whether at twenty or eighty. Anyone who keeps learning stays young. The greatest thing in life is to keep your mind young.

Henry Ford

Cultivate in yourself the qualities you admire most in others.

Arnold Glason

People seldom improve when they have no other model but themselves to copy after.

Goldsmith

Learning is acquired by reading books, but the much more necessary learning, the knowledge of the world, is only to be acquired by reading men, and studying all the various facets of them.

Lord Chesterfield

No man can really be big who does not read widely outside his own field.

Theodore N. Vail

Read every day something no one else is reading. Think every day something no one else is thinking. It is bad for the mind to be always a part of unanimity.

Christopher Morley

Today a reader, tomorrow a leader.

W. Fusselman

The trouble with most of us is we would rather be ruined by praise than saved by criticism.

Dr. Norman Vincent Peale

You cannot run away from a weakness. You must sometimes fight it out or perish; and if that be so, why not now, and where you stand?

Robert Louis Stevenson

31

Success Is...

Success is being at peace with yourself.

Success is where preparation and opportunity meet.

Bobby Unser

    You can use most any measure when you're speaking of success.
    You can measure it in a fancy home, expensive car or dress.
    But the measure of your real success is one you cannot spend—
    It's the way your child describes you when talking to a friend.

Martin Baxbaum

You have reached the pinnacle of success as soon as you become uninterested in money, compliments or publicity.
Dr. O. A. Battista

Success in life has nothing to do with what you gain in life or accomplish for yourself. It's what you do for others.
Danny Thomas

The man who lives for himself is a failure; the man who lives for others has achieved true success.
Dr. Norman Vincent Peale

Any man who is honest, fair, tolerant, kindly, charitable of others and well behaved is a success, no matter what his station in life.

Jay E. House

If a man lives a decent life and does his work fairly and squarely so that those dependent upon him and attached to him are better for his having lived, then he is success.

Theodore Roosevelt

Success is a journey, not a destination.

Ben Sweetland

Real Success in business is to be found in achievements comparable rather with those of the artist or the scientist, or the inventor or the statesman. And the joys sought in the profession of business must be like their joys and not the mere vulgar satisfaction which is experienced in the acquisition of money, in the exercise of power, or in the frivolous pleasure of mere winning.

Justice Louis D. Brandeis

32

Requirements
For Success

He who wishes to fulfill his mission in the world must be a man of one idea, that is, of one great overmastering purpose, overshadowing all his aims, and guiding and controlling his entire life.

Bate

Nothing is as necessary for success as the single minded pursuit of an objective.
Frederick W. Smith

The first and most important step toward success is the feeling that we can succeed.
Nelson Boswell

The winners in life think constantly in terms of I can, I will and I am. Losers, on the other hand, concentrate their waking thoughts on what they should have done, or what they don't do.

Dennis Waitley

The only thing that stands between a man and what he wants from life is often merely the will to try it and the faith to believe that it is possible.

Richard M. Devos

The key to success is holding in your conscious mind what you want to achieve and then striving in everything you do to make the image reality.

Dr. Norman Vincent Peale

The starting point of all achievement is desire.

Napoleon Hill

The will to persevere is often the difference between failure and success.

David Sarnoff

The people who succeed are the few who have the ambition and the willpower to develop themselves.

Herbert Casson

251

If one advances confidently in the direction of his dreams, and endeavors to live the life which he has imagined, he will meet with success unexpected in common hours.

Henry David Thoreau

We're worn into grooves by time—by our habits. In the end, these grooves are going to show whether we've been second rate or champions.

Frank B. Gilberth

Success is not due to a fortuitous concourse of stars at our birth, but to a steady trial of sparks from the grindstone of hard work each day.

Kenneth Hildebrand

Luck is a dividend of sweat. The more you sweat, the luckier you get.

Ray Kroc

He who would accomplish little must sacrifice little; he who would achieve much must sacrifice much.

James Allen

The future belongs to those who are willing to make short-term sacrifices for long-term gains.

Fred A. Manske, Sr.

There is no success without hardship.
Sophocles

Great men are little men expanded; great lives are ordinary lives intensified.
Wilfred A. Peterson

Experience shows that success is due less to ability than to zeal. The winner is he who gives himself to his work, body and soul.
Charles Buxton

Everything comes to him who hustles while he waits.
Thomas Edison

Success requires that you push yourself beyond your comfort zone.

Unless a man undertakes more than he possibly can do, he will never do all he can do.

Henry Drummond

The right man is the one who seizes the moment.

Goethe

255

I should never have made my success in life if I had not bestowed upon the least thing I have ever undertaken the same attention and care that I bestowed upon the greatest.

Charles Dickens

The difference between failure and success is doing a thing nearly right and doing a thing exactly right.

Edward Simmons

Paying attention to simple little things that most men neglect makes a few men rich.
Henry Ford

The only certain measure of success is to render more and better service than is expected of you.

O. G. Mandino

Make service your first priority, not success, and success will follow.

Try not to become a man of success but rather try to become a man of value.

Albert Einstein

The winds and the waves are always on the side of the ablest navigators.

Edward Gibbon

It's no exaggeration to say that a strong positive self-image is the best possible preparation for success in life.

Dr. Joyce Brothers

Six essential qualities are the key to success: sincerity, personal integrity, humility, courtesy, wisdom, charity.

Dr. William Menninger

The ability to form friendships, to make people believe in you and trust you, is one of the few absolutely fundamental qualities of success.

John J. McGuirk

The key to executive success is the ability to inspire teamwork.

Henry L. Doherty

There is no limit to what a man can do or where he can go if he doesn't mind who gets the credit.

Author Unknown

If you do not think about the future and prepare for it, you will not have one.

Most people don't succeed in life because they don't know what they want to achieve in the first place.

A man without a purpose is like a ship without a rudder.

Thomas Carlyle

The world stands aside to let anyone pass who knows where he is going.

David Starr Gordon

Never look down to test the ground before taking your next step; only he who keeps his eyes fixed on the far horizon will find his right road.

Dag Hammarskjöld

You've removed most of the road-blocks to success when you've learn't the difference between motion and direction.

Bill Copeland

If you want to succeed you should strike out on new paths rather than travel the worn paths of accepted success.

John D. Rockefeller, Jr.

The man who goes farthest is generally the one who is willing to do and dare. The sure-thing boat never gets far from shore.

Dale Carnegie

Only those who dare to fail greatly can ever achieve greatly.

Robert F. Kennedy

He who dares nothing, need hope for nothing.

Johann Schiller

The secret of success in life is for a person to be ready for opportunity when it comes.
Benjamin Disraeli

To know how to wait is one of the great secrets of success.
James DeMaistre

Few people succeed in business unless they enjoy their work.

No man can deliver the goods if his heart is heavier than the load.
Frank Irving Fletcher

He who would climb the ladder must begin at the bottom.

English Proverb

Do not waste a minute — not a second — in trying to demonstrate to others the merits of your performance. If your work does not indicate itself, you cannot vindicate it.

Thomas W. Higginson

Nothing succeeds like success.

Alexandre Dumas

Hitch your wagon to a star.

Ralph Waldo Emerson

ALSO AVAILABLE

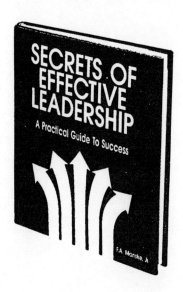

YOUR GUIDE TO SUCCESS

PRACTICAL IDEAS ON HOW TO:

Build Group Pride and Morale
Inspire Employees
Hold People Accountable
Bring New Focus and Energy To Your Job
Manage Stress and Avoid Burnout
Improve Your Weaknesses

PLUS:

Leadership Self-Appraisal
Special Section On How To Reach
Your Full Leadership Potential
The 10 Commandments of Leadership

EADERSHIP EDUCATION AND DEVELOPMENT, INC.
P.O. BOX 382007, GERMANTOWN, TN. 38138-2007

INDEX